THE STARTUP SAVANT

Insider Tips for Launching and Scaling Your Business

NANCY BARLOW

Copyright © 2024 by Nancy Barlow

TABLE OF CONTENT

INTRODUCTION

In the vast and ever-evolving landscape of entrepreneurship, navigating the turbulent waters of launching and scaling a business can often feel like embarking on an odyssey without a map. The journey is fraught with challenges, uncertainties, and a myriad of decisions that can make or break the fate of a startup. However, amidst this chaos lies a beacon of hope – the wisdom and insights of seasoned entrepreneurs who have braved the storm and emerged victorious.

Welcome to "The Startup Savant: Insider Tips for Launching and Scaling Your Business," a comprehensive guide crafted for aspiring and established entrepreneurs alike, seeking to carve their path to success in the competitive world of business. Written with the belief that knowledge is the most powerful asset one can possess on the entrepreneurial journey, this book serves as a compass, guiding you through the intricate maze of startup challenges while equipping you with the tools and strategies necessary to thrive.

Drawing upon years of experience, industry expertise, and firsthand insights from successful entrepreneurs and business leaders, "The Startup Savant" is more than just a manual – it's a roadmap meticulously designed to empower you at every stage of your entrepreneurial voyage. Whether you're a budding entrepreneur with a groundbreaking idea or a seasoned business owner aiming to expand your empire, this book offers practical advice, actionable steps, and invaluable lessons learned from the trenches of startup warfare.

From crafting a compelling business plan to securing funding, from building a standout brand to mastering the art of effective leadership, each chapter is meticulously curated to address key challenges encountered by entrepreneurs across industries. Through real-world case studies, expert interviews, and proven strategies, you'll discover the secrets to unlocking your entrepreneurial potential and steering your venture towards sustainable growth and success.

"The Startup Savant" is not just a book – it's a mentor, a confidant, and a trusted ally on your entrepreneurial journey. So, buckle up and get ready to embark on a transformative odyssey towards building a thriving business that defies the odds and leaves a lasting legacy in the annals of entrepreneurship.

CHAPTER 1: SETTING THE STAGE

Embarking on the journey of entrepreneurship is akin to stepping onto a grand stage, with the spotlight shining brightly upon you. But before the curtains rise and the audience applauds, there's a crucial phase that every entrepreneur must undergo – setting the stage for success. In this pivotal chapter, we delve deep into the foundational aspects of entrepreneurship, providing you with the insights and tools necessary to lay a solid groundwork for your venture.

The entrepreneurial landscape is vast and dynamic, characterized by both boundless opportunities and daunting challenges. Understanding this terrain is paramount, as it allows you to navigate the twists and turns of the journey with clarity and purpose. We'll explore the intricacies of market dynamics, helping you identify lucrative opportunities and potential pitfalls that lie ahead.

But embarking on the entrepreneurial journey isn't merely about seizing opportunities; it's also about self-awareness and preparedness. Are you truly ready to take the plunge into the world of entrepreneurship? We'll guide you through a process of introspection, helping you assess your skills, mindset, and readiness for the challenges that lie ahead.

As you embark on this transformative journey, remember that setting the stage is about more than just laying a foundation – it's about igniting a spark of passion, vision, and resilience that will fuel your entrepreneurial endeavors. So, as we embark on this chapter together, let us embrace the excitement and uncertainty that comes with setting the stage for entrepreneurial success.

- Understanding the Entrepreneurial Landscape

The entrepreneurial landscape is a dynamic and multifaceted ecosystem that encompasses a wide array of opportunities, challenges, and stakeholders. It is characterized by its fluidity, constantly evolving in response to technological advancements, economic fluctuations, regulatory changes, and shifting consumer preferences. Understanding the nuances of this landscape is essential for entrepreneurs seeking to navigate its complexities and capitalize on emerging opportunities. Let's comprehensively discuss the key elements that define the entrepreneurial landscape:

1. **Market Dynamics:**

 - **Market size and growth potential:** Entrepreneurs must assess the size of their target market and its growth trajectory to gauge the viability of their business idea.

- **Industry trends and disruptors:** Keeping abreast of industry trends and potential disruptors is crucial for identifying opportunities and staying ahead of the competition.

- **Competitive landscape:** Understanding competitors' strengths, weaknesses, and market positioning enables entrepreneurs to differentiate their offerings and carve out a niche.

2. **Technological Innovation:**

- **Rapid technological advancements:** Technologies such as artificial intelligence, blockchain, and the Internet of Things are reshaping industries and creating new business opportunities.

- **Disruptive innovation:** Entrepreneurs must embrace disruptive technologies and innovative business models to stay relevant in an increasingly competitive landscape.

- **Access to technology**: The democratization of technology has lowered barriers to entry, allowing entrepreneurs to leverage tools and platforms to launch and scale their ventures more efficiently.

3. Funding and Investment:

- **Funding options**: Entrepreneurs can access a variety of funding sources, including bootstrapping, angel investors, venture capital, crowdfunding, and government grants.

- **Investor expectations:** Understanding investor expectations and requirements is crucial for securing funding and building investor confidence.

- **Funding landscape:** The availability of funding varies across regions and industries, with certain sectors attracting more investment than others.

4. Regulatory Environment:

- **Compliance requirements**: Entrepreneurs must navigate a complex web of regulations and compliance standards, which vary depending on factors such as industry, location, and business model.

  - **Regulatory barriers to entry:** Regulatory hurdles can pose challenges for startups, requiring entrepreneurs to invest time and resources in navigating legal and regulatory frameworks.

  - **Policy and advocacy:** Engaging with policymakers and industry stakeholders can help entrepreneurs shape regulatory policies and create a more conducive environment for innovation and entrepreneurship.

5. Cultural and Social Factors:

  - **Entrepreneurial culture:** Cultural attitudes towards risk-taking, failure, and entrepreneurship influence the prevalence and success of startups within a society.

  - **Support networks:** Access to mentorship, networking opportunities, and entrepreneurial support programs can enhance the likelihood of startup success.

- **Social impact:** Increasingly, entrepreneurs are incorporating social and environmental considerations into their business models, aligning their ventures with values-driven consumers and investors.

In conclusion, the entrepreneurial landscape is a dynamic and multifaceted ecosystem shaped by market dynamics, technological innovation, funding and investment, regulatory environments, and cultural and social factors. Entrepreneurs must navigate these complexities with agility, resilience, and a keen understanding of the opportunities and challenges that define the entrepreneurial journey. By embracing change, harnessing innovation, and leveraging available resources, entrepreneurs can thrive in this ever-evolving landscape and create impactful ventures that drive economic growth and societal change.

- Identifying Market Opportunities

Identifying market opportunities is a crucial step in the entrepreneurial journey, as it lays the foundation for the success of a business venture. This process involves systematically analyzing the market landscape to uncover unmet needs, emerging trends, and gaps in the market that can be exploited for competitive advantage. Let's comprehensively discuss the steps involved in identifying market opportunities:

1. **Market Research:**

   - Conduct thorough market research to gain insights into the size, growth, and dynamics of the target market.

   - Identify key market segments and demographics to understand the needs, preferences, and behaviors of potential customers.

- Analyze market trends, industry reports, and competitor strategies to identify emerging opportunities and areas of growth.

2. **Customer Discovery:**

- Engage in customer discovery interviews, surveys, and focus groups to gather firsthand insights from potential customers.

- Identify pain points, challenges, and unmet needs that customers are experiencing within the market.

- Validate assumptions and hypotheses through iterative feedback loops with target customers, refining the understanding of market opportunities based on real-world insights.

3. **SWOT Analysis:**

- Conduct a SWOT (Strengths, Weaknesses, Opportunities, Threats) analysis to assess the internal and external factors influencing the business environment.

- Identify strengths and competitive advantages that can be leveraged to capitalize on market opportunities.

- Identify weaknesses and threats that may pose challenges or hinder the pursuit of identified opportunities.

4. Emerging Trends and Technologies:

- Stay abreast of emerging trends, technologies, and industry disruptions that may create new market opportunities.

- Monitor changes in consumer behavior, preferences, and purchasing patterns driven by technological advancements and societal shifts.

- Anticipate future market needs and demands by forecasting the impact of emerging trends on consumer behavior and industry dynamics.

5. Gap Analysis:

- Identify gaps in the market where demand exceeds supply or existing solutions fail to adequately address customer needs.

- Evaluate existing products, services, and solutions in the market to identify areas of improvement or innovation.

- Explore adjacent markets and industries for untapped opportunities that align with the core competencies and capabilities of the business.

6. **Competitive Analysis:**

- Analyze the competitive landscape to understand the strengths, weaknesses, and strategies of existing players in the market.

- Identify underserved or overlooked market segments where competitors are less active or effective.

- Differentiate the business by offering unique value propositions, innovative solutions, or superior customer experiences that resonate with target customers.

7. **Market Validation:**

- Validate market opportunities through pilot tests, prototype development, or MVP (Minimum Viable

Product) launches to assess market demand and customer response.

- Gather feedback, metrics, and performance data to evaluate the viability and scalability of identified opportunities.

- Iterate and refine market opportunities based on real-world validation and ongoing market feedback.

In conclusion, identifying market opportunities is a systematic process that involves rigorous research, customer discovery, SWOT analysis, monitoring emerging trends, gap analysis, competitive analysis, and market validation. By understanding market dynamics, customer needs, and competitive landscapes, entrepreneurs can uncover untapped opportunities, innovate with confidence, and position their ventures for sustainable growth and success in an ever-evolving marketplace.

- Assessing Your Readiness for Entrepreneurship

Assessing your readiness for entrepreneurship is a critical step before embarking on the entrepreneurial journey. It involves introspection, self-assessment, and evaluation of your skills, mindset, resources, and motivations to determine whether you possess the necessary attributes and capabilities to succeed as an entrepreneur. Let's comprehensively discuss the process of assessing your readiness for entrepreneurship:

1. Self-Reflection:

- Reflect on your strengths, weaknesses, passions, and interests to gain clarity on your entrepreneurial aspirations.

- Assess your personal and professional goals, values, and priorities to ensure alignment with the demands and challenges of entrepreneurship.

- Evaluate your tolerance for risk, uncertainty, and ambiguity, considering the inherent volatility of the entrepreneurial journey.

2. Skills and Competencies:

- Identify the skills, knowledge, and competencies required to launch and manage a successful business.

- Assess your proficiency in areas such as leadership, communication, problem-solving, decision-making, financial management, marketing, and sales.

- Identify gaps in your skill set and develop a plan to acquire or strengthen essential skills through education, training, or mentorship.

3. Financial Preparedness:

- Evaluate your financial situation, including savings, investments, debts, and financial obligations, to determine your readiness to withstand the financial challenges of entrepreneurship.

- Assess your ability to secure funding or financing for your business venture through personal savings, loans, investments, or external sources of capital.

- Develop a realistic budget, financial projections, and contingency plans to mitigate financial risks and ensure the sustainability of your business.

4. **Support Network:**

- Assess the strength and diversity of your support network, including family, friends, mentors, advisors, and professional contacts.

- Seek feedback, guidance, and advice from experienced entrepreneurs and industry experts to gain insights into the realities of entrepreneurship and enhance your readiness.

- Build relationships with potential collaborators, partners, suppliers, and customers to leverage resources and opportunities for your business venture.

5. Motivation and Resilience:

- Evaluate your level of motivation, passion, and commitment to pursue entrepreneurship despite the inevitable challenges, setbacks, and failures.

- Assess your ability to adapt, pivot, and persevere in the face of adversity, uncertainty, and unexpected obstacles.

- Cultivate a growth mindset, resilience, and a positive attitude to overcome challenges and maintain momentum on your entrepreneurial journey.

6. Lifestyle Considerations:

- Consider the impact of entrepreneurship on your lifestyle, personal relationships, health, and well-being.

- Assess your ability to manage work-life balance, stress, and burnout while pursuing entrepreneurial endeavors.

- Identify strategies for self-care, time management, and prioritization to maintain physical, mental, and emotional health throughout the entrepreneurial journey.

7. **Commitment to Continuous Learning:**

   - Recognize the importance of lifelong learning and professional development in entrepreneurship.

   - Assess your willingness to embrace new challenges, acquire new skills, and adapt to evolving market dynamics and industry trends.

   - Commit to continuous learning, experimentation, and improvement to enhance your entrepreneurial capabilities and increase your chances of success.

In conclusion, assessing your readiness for entrepreneurship is a comprehensive process that involves self-reflection, skills assessment, financial preparedness, building a support network, cultivating motivation and resilience, considering lifestyle implications, and committing to continuous learning and growth. By critically evaluating your readiness and addressing any gaps or challenges proactively, you can increase your confidence, preparedness, and chances of success as you embark on the entrepreneurial journey.

CHAPTER 2: BUILDING THE FOUNDATION

In the journey of entrepreneurship, success is not solely defined by the brilliance of an idea or the determination of its founder. Instead, it hinges upon the strength of the foundation upon which the venture is built. Chapter 2: Building the Foundation is where we delve into the essential groundwork necessary to establish a robust and resilient business.

Building a successful business is akin to constructing a sturdy edifice. It requires careful planning, meticulous attention to detail, and a solid framework that can withstand the tests of time and adversity. In this chapter, we explore the critical elements that form the bedrock of any thriving enterprise, from crafting a compelling business plan to defining a unique value proposition and conducting comprehensive market research.

A well-crafted business plan serves as the blueprint for your venture, guiding your strategic decisions and outlining the path to success. We delve into the intricacies of developing a business plan that not only articulates your vision and goals but also addresses key components such as market analysis, competitive positioning, financial projections, and growth strategies.

Central to the foundation of any successful business is a clear and compelling value proposition. We discuss the importance of defining what sets your product or service apart from the competition and how to communicate its unique benefits to your target audience effectively. By understanding the needs, desires, and pain points of your customers, you can tailor your value proposition to resonate with their preferences and drive demand for your offerings.

Additionally, we emphasize the significance of conducting thorough market research to gain insights into your target market, identify growth opportunities, and mitigate potential risks. By analyzing market trends, customer behavior, and competitive dynamics, you can make informed decisions that position your business for success in a competitive marketplace.

As we embark on this journey of building the foundation for your venture, remember that every brick laid and every decision made will shape the trajectory of your business. By investing time and effort in laying a solid foundation, you set the stage for sustainable growth, resilience, and success in the ever-evolving landscape of entrepreneurship. So, let us roll up our sleeves and begin the process of building the foundation for your entrepreneurial dreams.

- Crafting a Compelling Business Plan

Crafting a compelling business plan is a foundational step in the entrepreneurial journey, providing a roadmap for the venture's growth and success. A well-developed business plan not only serves as a strategic tool for guiding decision-making but also communicates the viability and potential of the business to stakeholders such as investors, partners, and employees. Let's comprehensively discuss the process of crafting a compelling business plan:

1. **Executive Summary:**

- Provide a concise overview of the business concept, objectives, and value proposition.

- Summarize key components of the business plan, including market analysis, competitive positioning, revenue model, and financial projections.

- Highlight the unique selling points and competitive advantages of the venture to capture the reader's attention and interest.

2. **Company Description:**

- Provide background information on the business, including its history, mission, vision, and core values.

- Describe the products or services offered, target market, and competitive landscape.

- Outline the legal structure, ownership, and management team of the company.

3. Market Analysis:

- Conduct thorough market research to identify target market segments, customer demographics, and purchasing behavior.

- Analyze industry trends, market size, growth potential, and competitive dynamics.

- Assess market gaps, unmet needs, and opportunities for differentiation or innovation.

4. Competitive Analysis:

- Identify direct and indirect competitors operating within the target market.

- Evaluate competitors' strengths, weaknesses, market positioning, and pricing strategies.

- Highlight the unique value proposition and competitive advantages that differentiate the business from competitors.

5. Customer Segmentation and Targeting:

- Segment the target market based on demographic, psychographic, geographic, or behavioral criteria.

- Identify target customer personas, including their needs, preferences, pain points, and purchasing behavior.

- Define the primary and secondary target markets and tailor marketing strategies to address their specific needs and preferences.

6. Marketing and Sales Strategy:

- Outline the marketing channels, tactics, and campaigns used to reach target customers and generate demand.

- Define the pricing strategy, including pricing tiers, discounts, and promotional offers.

- Describe the sales process, distribution channels, and customer acquisition strategy.

7. **Operational Plan:**

- Describe the operational structure, facilities, equipment, and technology required to support business operations.

- Outline key operational processes, workflow, and quality control measures.

- Address staffing needs, recruitment strategies, and employee training and development plans.

8. **Financial Projections:**

- Prepare comprehensive financial projections, including income statements, cash flow forecasts, and balance sheets.

- Estimate revenue projections, expenses, and profitability over the short-term and long term.

- Conduct sensitivity analysis and scenario planning to assess the impact of various factors on financial performance.

9. Risk Management and Contingency Planning:

- Identify potential risks, challenges, and uncertainties that may impact the business.

- Develop risk mitigation strategies, contingency plans, and alternative courses of action.

- Address regulatory compliance, legal risks, cybersecurity threats, and market volatility.

10. Conclusion:

- Summarize the key findings, insights, and recommendations outlined in the business plan.

- Reiterate the value proposition, competitive advantages, and growth potential of the business.

- Conclude with a compelling call to action, inviting stakeholders to engage with the business and support its growth objectives.

In conclusion, crafting a compelling business plan is a comprehensive process that involves conducting market research, analyzing competition, identifying target customers, developing marketing and sales strategies, outlining operational plans, preparing financial projections, and addressing risk management considerations. By meticulously documenting the business concept, strategies, and financial forecasts, entrepreneurs can articulate a compelling vision and secure support from stakeholders to propel their ventures towards success.

- Defining Your Unique Value Proposition

Defining your unique value proposition (UVP) is a critical step in the process of building a successful business. Your UVP articulates the specific value that your product or service offers to customers and distinguishes your brand from competitors in the marketplace. It answers the fundamental question: "Why should customers choose your offering over alternatives?" Let's comprehensively discuss the process of defining your unique value proposition:

1. **Market Research:**

  - Conduct thorough market research to understand the needs, preferences, and pain points of your target audience.

  - Identify existing solutions and competitors in the market, analyzing their strengths, weaknesses, and positioning.

  - Explore customer feedback, reviews, and testimonials to gain insights into the factors that influence purchasing decisions.

2. **Identify Customer Benefits:**

  - Identify the primary benefits or outcomes that customers seek when addressing their needs or solving their problems.

  - Consider both tangible benefits (e.g., cost savings, convenience, efficiency) and intangible benefits (e.g., status, prestige, peace of mind) that resonate with your target audience.

  - Prioritize customer benefits based on their importance and relevance to your target market.

3. Understand Differentiation:

- Assess how your product or service differs from competitors and addresses unmet needs or pain points in the market.

- Identify unique features, functionalities, or characteristics that set your offering apart and create value for customers.

- Consider how your brand's reputation, values, and customer experience contribute to differentiation and brand loyalty.

4. Define Your Value Proposition:

- Clearly articulate the specific value that your product or service delivers to customers concisely and compellingly.

- Focus on addressing the most critical customer needs or pain points with a clear and compelling promise of benefits.

- Use language that resonates with your target audience and communicates the unique advantages of your offering effectively.

- Ensure that your value proposition is clear, memorable, and easily understood by customers.

5. **Test and Refine:**

- Test different value propositions with target customers through surveys, interviews, or A/B testing to gather feedback and insights.

- Monitor customer reactions, engagement metrics, and sales data to evaluate the effectiveness of your value proposition.

- Iterate and refine your value proposition based on customer feedback, market trends, and competitive dynamics.

6. **Communicate Your Value Proposition:**

- Integrate your value proposition into all aspects of your marketing and branding efforts, including messaging, visuals, and customer touchpoints.

- Use storytelling, case studies, and testimonials to illustrate how your offering solves customer problems and delivers value.

- Continuously reinforce and communicate your value proposition through digital and traditional marketing channels to build brand awareness and attract customers.

7. **Align with Brand Strategy:**

- Ensure that your value proposition aligns with your brand's mission, values, and positioning in the market.

- Integrate your value proposition into your brand messaging, tagline, and brand identity to create a consistent and cohesive brand experience.

- Ensure that all stakeholders, including employees, partners, and customers, understand and resonate with your brand's unique value proposition.

In conclusion, defining your unique value proposition is a strategic process that involves understanding customer needs, identifying differentiation, articulating value, testing and refining, communicating effectively, and aligning with brand strategy. By clearly defining and communicating the specific value that your offering delivers to customers, you can differentiate your brand, attract loyal customers, and drive business growth in a competitive marketplace.

- Conducting Market Research and Analysis

Conducting market research and analysis is a crucial step in the entrepreneurial journey, providing valuable insights into the target market, customer needs, competitive landscape, and industry trends. This process involves gathering, analyzing, and interpreting data to inform strategic decision-making and validate business ideas. Let's comprehensively discuss the process of conducting market research and analysis:

1. **Define Objectives:**

   - Clearly define the objectives and goals of your market research to guide the process effectively.

   - Determine the specific questions you want to answer, such as identifying target customers, assessing market size, understanding competitors, or evaluating demand for a new product or service.

2. Identify Research Methods:

- Choose appropriate research methods and techniques based on your objectives, budget, and resources.

- Common market research methods include surveys, interviews, focus groups, observation, secondary research (using existing data and reports), and online analytics tools.

- Consider both qualitative and quantitative research approaches to gain comprehensive insights into the target market.

3. Define Target Market:

- Identify and define the target market segments that your business intends to serve.

- Segment the market based on demographic factors (e.g., age, gender, income), psychographic factors (e.g., lifestyle, values, attitudes), geographic location, or behavioral characteristics (e.g., purchasing behavior, usage patterns).

- Prioritize target market segments based on their size, growth potential, accessibility, and alignment with your business objectives.

4. Gather Data:

- Collect relevant data and information from primary and secondary sources to support your market research objectives.

- Primary data refers to data collected directly from target customers or stakeholders through surveys, interviews, or experiments.

- Secondary data refers to existing data and information obtained from sources such as government agencies, industry reports, academic research, or market intelligence platforms.

5. Analyze Data:

- Organize and analyze the collected data to derive meaningful insights and patterns.

- Use statistical analysis, data visualization tools, and qualitative coding techniques to interpret and synthesize the data effectively.

- Identify key trends, patterns, correlations, and outliers that provide insights into customer preferences, market dynamics, and competitive positioning.

6. **Assess Competitive Landscape:**

- Conduct a comprehensive analysis of the competitive landscape to understand the strengths, weaknesses, strategies, and market positioning of competitors.

- Identify direct and indirect competitors operating within the target market and assess their product offerings, pricing, distribution channels, and marketing strategies.

- Analyze competitor reviews, customer feedback, and online presence to identify opportunities for differentiation and competitive advantage.

7. **Interpret Findings:**

- Interpret the findings of your market research in the context of your business objectives and industry dynamics.

- Draw actionable insights and recommendations that inform strategic decision-making, product development, marketing strategies, and business planning.

- Consider implications for market segmentation, target positioning, pricing strategies, distribution channels, and customer acquisition tactics.

8. **Validate Assumptions:**

- Validate assumptions and hypotheses generated from market research through iterative testing and experimentation.

- Pilot test new products, features, or marketing campaigns with target customers to gather feedback and validate demand.

- Use market validation techniques such as MVP (Minimum Viable Product) launches, beta testing, or pre-orders to assess market response and refine business strategies accordingly.

9. Monitor Market Trends:

- Continuously monitor market trends, industry developments, and competitor actions to stay informed and adapt your strategies accordingly.

- Use market intelligence tools, industry reports, news sources, and social media monitoring to track changes in customer preferences, technology advancements, regulatory changes, and emerging opportunities or threats.

10. Iterate and Refine:

- Iterate and refine your market research and analysis process based on ongoing feedback, insights, and learnings.

- Incorporate new data, feedback, and market developments into your strategic planning process to ensure relevance and effectiveness.

- Continuously seek opportunities for improvement and optimization to enhance the accuracy, depth, and impact of your market research efforts.

In conclusion, conducting market research and analysis is a systematic process that involves defining objectives, selecting research methods, defining target markets, gathering data, analyzing findings, assessing the competitive landscape, interpreting insights, validating assumptions, monitoring trends, and iterating and refining continuously. By leveraging data-driven insights and market intelligence, entrepreneurs can make informed decisions, mitigate risks, capitalize on opportunities, and drive sustainable growth and success in their ventures.

CHAPTER 3: SECURING RESOURCES

In the entrepreneurial journey, securing resources is akin to gathering the necessary tools and materials before embarking on a construction project. Just as a builder requires lumber, nails, and cement, entrepreneurs need access to capital, expertise, and support to bring their vision to life. Chapter 3: Securing Resources explores the diverse array of resources available to entrepreneurs and provides strategies for accessing and leveraging them effectively.

Securing resources is a critical aspect of entrepreneurship, as it enables founders to transform their ideas into viable businesses and navigate the challenges of startup growth. Whether it's funding to fuel expansion, mentorship to provide guidance, or access to networks to facilitate partnerships, the availability and utilization of resources can make or break the success of a venture.

In this chapter, we delve into the various avenues through which entrepreneurs can secure the resources needed to launch, grow, and scale their businesses. From bootstrapping and self-funding to seeking investment from angel investors and venture capitalists, we explore the diverse range of funding options available to startups at different stages of development.

Additionally, we examine the importance of building a support network and accessing mentorship to navigate the complexities of entrepreneurship. By tapping into the expertise and experience of seasoned entrepreneurs, advisors, and industry experts, founders can gain valuable insights, avoid common pitfalls, and accelerate their growth trajectory.

Furthermore, we explore alternative sources of funding and support, such as government grants, incubators, accelerators, and crowdfunding platforms. These resources provide valuable opportunities for startups to access capital, mentorship, and networking opportunities while minimizing dilution of ownership and control.

As we embark on this exploration of securing resources, it's essential to recognize that entrepreneurship is not a solitary endeavor. By leveraging the collective wisdom, expertise, and resources available within the entrepreneurial ecosystem, founders can overcome challenges, seize opportunities, and realize their vision for a thriving and impactful business.

So, join us as we uncover the strategies, tactics, and resources necessary to secure the building blocks of entrepreneurial success. Whether you're a first-time founder with a groundbreaking idea or a seasoned entrepreneur aiming to take your business to new heights, this chapter will equip you with the tools and insights needed to secure the resources that will fuel your journey towards success.

- Exploring Funding Options: From Bootstrapping to Venture Capital

Funding options for startups vary widely, ranging from bootstrapping and self-funding to seeking investment from angel investors, venture capitalists (VCs), and other sources. Each funding option has its advantages, disadvantages, and suitability depending on the stage of the startup, its growth trajectory, and the entrepreneur's goals and preferences. Let's comprehensively discuss the various funding options available to startups:

1. **Bootstrapping and Self-Funding:**

   - Bootstrapping involves funding the startup using personal savings, credit cards, or revenue generated from the business.

- **Advantages:** Retain full ownership and control, avoid dilution of equity, maintain flexibility and independence, and minimize debt and interest payments.

- **Disadvantages**: Limited initial capital may restrict growth and scalability, increased personal financial risk, slower growth trajectory compared to funded startups.

2. Friends and Family:

- Seeking investment from friends and family members can provide early-stage capital to launch or grow the startup.

- **Advantages:** Access to capital with fewer strings attached, potential for lower interest rates or favorable repayment terms, ability to leverage personal relationships and trust.

- **Disadvantages:** Strain on personal relationships if the business fails, potential for conflicts of interest or disagreements over financial terms, limited access to larger funding rounds.

3. Angel Investors:

- Angel investors are affluent individuals who provide capital to startups in exchange for equity ownership.

- **Advantages:** Access to experienced mentors and advisors, smaller funding rounds with faster decision-making compared to VCs, potential for strategic partnerships and introductions to other investors.

- **Disadvantages:** Limited capital compared to VCs, the potential for less stringent due diligence and oversight, alignment of interests with individual investors may vary.

4. Venture Capital:

- Venture capital firms invest institutional funds in high-growth startups with the potential for significant returns.

- **Advantages:** Access to larger amounts of capital for rapid growth and scaling, expertise in scaling startups, and access to extensive networks of investors, advisors, and potential customers.

- **Disadvantages:** Dilution of ownership and control, high expectations for growth and profitability, rigorous due diligence and reporting requirements, potential for conflicts with investors over strategic direction.

5. Crowdfunding:

- Crowdfunding platforms allow startups to raise capital from a large number of individuals or investors through online campaigns.

- **Advantages:** Access to capital without giving up equity, validation of product or market demand, potential for marketing and exposure, ability to engage with early adopters and brand advocates.

- **Disadvantages:** Time-consuming to prepare and manage crowdfunding campaigns, fees and commissions charged by crowdfunding platforms, and regulatory compliance requirements vary by jurisdiction.

6. **Corporate Venture Capital (CVC):**

- Corporate venture capital refers to investment funds established by corporations to invest in startups that align with their strategic objectives.

- **Advantages:** Access to capital and strategic partnerships with established corporations, the potential for product development, distribution, and market access, validation of market potential and scalability.

- **Disadvantages:** Potential conflicts of interest or control issues, alignment of interests with corporate objectives, potential for conflicts over strategic direction or intellectual property rights.

7. **Government Grants and Incentives:**

- Governments offer grants, subsidies, tax incentives, and other financial support programs to stimulate entrepreneurship and innovation.

- **Advantages:** Non-dilutive funding that does not require equity stake, the potential for financial support for R&D, innovation, and job creation, eligibility criteria vary by jurisdiction.

   - **Disadvantages:** Competitive application process, restrictions on the use of funds, reporting and compliance requirements, limited availability and funding amounts.

In conclusion, startups have a wide range of funding options available, each with its unique advantages, disadvantages, and suitability depending on the stage of the startup, growth trajectory, and founder's goals and preferences. By understanding the characteristics and implications of each funding option, entrepreneurs can make informed decisions and secure the capital needed to fuel their growth and success.

- Navigating the World of Angel Investors and Crowdfunding

Navigating the world of angel investors and crowdfunding involves understanding the nuances of these funding sources, building relationships, and effectively communicating your startup's value proposition to potential investors or backers. Both angel investors and crowdfunding platforms provide avenues for startups to raise capital, but each has its unique characteristics, advantages, and challenges. Let's comprehensively discuss the process of navigating the world of angel investors and crowdfunding:

1. Understanding Angel Investors:

- Angel investors are affluent individuals who provide capital to startups in exchange for equity ownership.

- Research and identify potential angel investors who have experience or interest in your industry, stage of development, or geographic location.

- Attend networking events, pitch competitions, and industry conferences to meet and connect with angel investors.

- Tailor your pitch and messaging to resonate with the interests, preferences, and investment criteria of angel investors, focusing on the potential for high returns and the scalability of your business.

2. **Building Relationships:**

- Cultivate relationships with angel investors through networking, introductions, and personalized outreach.

- Engage with potential investors by sharing updates, progress milestones, and opportunities for collaboration.

- Demonstrate transparency, integrity, and professionalism in your interactions with angel investors to build trust and credibility.

- Leverage existing connections, mentors, advisors, and industry contacts to access warm introductions and endorsements from reputable individuals.

3. Crafting a Compelling Pitch:

- Develop a compelling pitch deck that highlights the problem you're solving, your unique value proposition, market opportunity, traction, team, and financial projections.

- Clearly articulate the investment opportunity, including the potential for high returns, scalability, and competitive advantage.

- Tailor your pitch to address the specific interests, concerns, and investment criteria of angel investors, emphasizing alignment with their expertise and portfolio focus.

4. Negotiating Terms:

- Negotiate investment terms and terms sheets with angel investors, including valuation, equity stake, board representation, governance rights, and exit strategies.

- Seek legal advice and guidance to ensure that the terms are fair, equitable, and aligned with the long-term interests of the startup and its founders.

- Maintain open communication and transparency throughout the negotiation process, addressing any concerns or questions raised by angel investors promptly and professionally.

5. Understanding Crowdfunding Platforms:

- Crowdfunding platforms enable startups to raise capital from a large number of individuals or backers through online campaigns.

- Research and evaluate crowdfunding platforms based on their target audience, industry focus, fees, success rates, and track record.

- Choose the most appropriate crowdfunding model (e.g., rewards-based, equity-based, debt-based) based on your funding goals, regulatory considerations, and investor preferences.

6. **Planning and Launching Campaign:**

- Prepare and plan for a crowdfunding campaign, including setting funding goals, creating compelling campaign content, and designing attractive rewards or incentives for backers.

- Leverage storytelling, videos, visuals, and testimonials to communicate your startup's mission, value proposition, and impact to potential backers.

- Develop a marketing and promotion strategy to drive traffic, engagement, and contributions to your crowdfunding campaign, leveraging social media, email marketing, and PR outreach.

7. **Engaging with Backers:**

- Engage with backers and supporters throughout the crowdfunding campaign, responding to inquiries, providing updates, and expressing gratitude for their contributions.

- Cultivate a sense of community and belonging among backers, fostering loyalty, advocacy, and ongoing support for your startup beyond the campaign.

- Fulfill rewards or incentives promptly and transparently, maintaining open communication and addressing any issues or concerns raised by backers.

8. **Compliance and Regulatory Considerations:**

- Ensure compliance with applicable securities regulations, crowdfunding laws, and disclosure requirements when raising capital through crowdfunding platforms.

- Understand the legal and regulatory obligations associated with different crowdfunding models (e.g., equity crowdfunding, debt crowdfunding) and jurisdictions.

- Seek legal counsel and guidance to navigate regulatory complexities, protect intellectual property rights, and ensure compliance with securities laws and regulations.

9. **Managing Expectations:**

- Manage expectations of angel investors and crowdfunding backers by providing realistic projections, timelines, and milestones for the startup.

- Communicate transparently and proactively about progress, challenges, and setbacks encountered during the fundraising process and beyond.

- Demonstrate accountability, integrity, and a commitment to delivering on promises made to investors and backers, fostering trust and confidence in the startup's leadership team.

In conclusion, navigating the world of angel investors and crowdfunding requires strategic planning, relationship-building, effective communication, and compliance with legal and regulatory requirements. By understanding the characteristics and dynamics of each funding source, entrepreneurs can access the capital needed to fuel their growth and success while building relationships and communities of support that contribute to the long-term sustainability and impact of their startups.

- Leveraging Grants and Government Programs

Leveraging grants and government programs is a valuable strategy for startups and small businesses to access non-dilutive funding, resources, and support to fuel their growth and innovation initiatives. Government agencies, at both the federal and state levels, offer a variety of grants, incentives, and programs designed to stimulate economic development, promote entrepreneurship, and address societal challenges. Let's comprehensively discuss the process of leveraging grants and government programs:

1. **Research and Identify Opportunities:**

   - Conduct research to identify grants, incentives, and government programs that align with your business objectives, industry focus, and stage of development.

- Explore government agency websites, funding databases, and industry associations to identify relevant funding opportunities and eligibility criteria.

- Consider the specific needs and priorities of your business, such as R&D, innovation, job creation, export expansion, or sustainability initiatives, when evaluating potential programs.

2. **Understand Eligibility Requirements:**

- Review the eligibility criteria, guidelines, and application requirements for each grant or government program to determine if your business qualifies.

- Pay attention to factors such as business size, industry focus, geographic location, ownership structure, and project scope when assessing eligibility.

- Seek clarification from program administrators or funding agencies if you have questions or uncertainties about eligibility requirements or application procedures.

3. **Develop a Strong Proposal:**

- Develop a compelling grant proposal that clearly articulates the objectives, scope, and impact of your project or initiative.

- Align your proposal with the goals and priorities of the funding program, demonstrating how your project addresses identified needs or challenges.

- Provide detailed information on project goals, methodologies, timelines, budgets, and expected outcomes, using data and evidence to support your claims.

- Highlight the potential economic, social, or environmental benefits of your project, emphasizing its potential for job creation, innovation, or community impact.

4. Prepare Application Materials:

- Gather and prepare all required application materials, including forms, documents, certifications, and supporting evidence.

- Ensure that your application is complete, accurate, and compliant with all program requirements, paying attention to formatting, deadlines, and submission guidelines.

- Review your application materials carefully for errors, inconsistencies, and omissions before submitting them to the funding agency.

5. Submit Application and Follow-Up:

- Submit your grant application within the specified deadline, using the designated application portal or submission method specified by the funding agency.

- Keep track of your application status and follow up with the funding agency as needed to confirm receipt, address any questions or concerns, and track the progress of your application.

- Be prepared to provide additional information, clarification, or documentation if requested by the funding agency during the review process.

- Maintain open communication with program administrators or grant officers, responding promptly to any inquiries or requests for information.

6. **Fulfill Reporting and Compliance Obligations:**

- If awarded a grant or government funding, fulfil all reporting and compliance obligations outlined in the funding agreement or contract.

- Provide regular progress updates, financial reports, and performance metrics to the funding agency, demonstrating accountability and transparency in the use of grant funds.

- Comply with any specific requirements or conditions associated with the grant, such as hiring targets, project milestones, or environmental regulations.

- Seek guidance from program administrators or legal counsel if you encounter challenges or uncertainties regarding reporting or compliance obligations.

7. Explore Additional Resources and Support:

- Beyond financial assistance, government programs may offer additional resources, support services, and networking opportunities to help businesses succeed.

- Take advantage of training programs, workshops, mentoring, and advisory services offered by government agencies or partner organizations to enhance your business skills and capabilities.

- Engage with industry clusters, innovation hubs, and economic development organizations to access networking opportunities, market intelligence, and collaborative partnerships that can support your business growth initiatives.

In conclusion, leveraging grants and government programs requires careful research, strategic planning, and proactive engagement with funding agencies. By identifying relevant opportunities, understanding eligibility requirements, developing strong proposals, and fulfilling reporting and compliance obligations, startups and small businesses can access the non-dilutive funding and support needed to fuel their growth, innovation, and impact initiatives while contributing to economic development and societal progress.

CHAPTER 4: ESTABLISHING YOUR BRAND IDENTITY

In the competitive landscape of business, establishing a strong brand identity is essential for differentiation, recognition, and building trust with customers. Chapter 4: Establishing Your Brand Identity delves into the process of crafting a compelling brand identity that resonates with your target audience, communicates your values, and sets your business apart from competitors.

Your brand identity is more than just a logo or a tagline; it encompasses the entire perception and personality of your business. It encompasses the visual elements, messaging, tone of voice, values, and experiences that define how your brand is perceived by customers, stakeholders, and the wider market.

In this chapter, we explore the key components and strategies for building a distinct and memorable brand identity that captures the essence of your business and resonates with your target audience. From defining your brand values and personality to designing visual elements and crafting compelling messaging, we provide practical insights and actionable tips to help you establish a strong foundation for your brand.

Building a brand identity is not a one-time exercise but an ongoing process of evolution and refinement. It requires a deep understanding of your target market, competitive landscape, and industry trends, as well as a commitment to authenticity, consistency, and innovation.

Throughout this chapter, we'll explore the importance of brand positioning, differentiation, storytelling, and emotional connection in shaping perceptions and driving brand loyalty. We'll also discuss the role of digital marketing, social media, and customer engagement in amplifying your brand message and building meaningful relationships with your audience.

Whether you're a startup looking to make a memorable first impression or an established business seeking to refresh your brand identity, this chapter will provide you with the knowledge, tools, and inspiration to craft a compelling brand identity that resonates with your audience and sets you apart in the marketplace.

So, join us as we embark on a journey to establish your brand identity and unlock the power of storytelling, creativity, and authenticity to build a brand that leaves a lasting impression and drives business success.

- Developing a Memorable Brand Strategy

Developing a memorable brand strategy is a multifaceted process that involves defining your brand's purpose, values, personality, positioning, messaging, and visual identity. A well-crafted brand strategy serves as a blueprint for building a distinct and memorable brand that resonates with your target audience and differentiates your business from competitors. Let's comprehensively discuss the process of developing a memorable brand strategy:

1. Define Your Brand Purpose and Values:

- Start by defining the overarching purpose or mission of your brand, articulating why your business exists beyond making a profit.

- Identify and articulate the core values that guide your brand's decisions, behaviors, and interactions with customers, employees, and stakeholders.

- Ensure that your brand purpose and values are authentic, meaningful, and aligned with the aspirations and beliefs of your target audience.

2. Understand Your Target Audience:

- Conduct market research and audience analysis to gain insights into the demographics, psychographics, needs, preferences, and behaviors of your target audience.

- Develop detailed customer personas or profiles that represent your ideal customers, including their motivations, challenges, aspirations, and pain points.

- Use data-driven insights and customer feedback to refine your understanding of your target audience and tailor your brand strategy to address their needs effectively.

3. Establish Brand Positioning:

- Define your brand positioning by identifying the unique value proposition that sets your business apart from competitors and resonates with your target audience.

- Conduct a competitive analysis to assess the strengths, weaknesses, and market positioning of key competitors, identifying opportunities for differentiation and competitive advantage.

- Articulate your brand positioning statement, which succinctly communicates the unique benefits and value that your brand offers to customers about competitors.

4. Craft Compelling Brand Messaging:

- Develop a clear and compelling brand messaging framework that communicates your brand's story, values, benefits, and personality to your target audience.

- Define key brand messages, taglines, and value propositions that resonate with your audience and evoke an emotional connection.

- Tailor your messaging to different audience segments and communication channels, ensuring consistency and relevance across all touchpoints.

5. Design Visual Identity and Brand Assets:

- Create a cohesive visual identity that reflects your brand's personality, values, and positioning, including logo, color palette, typography, and imagery.

- Develop brand guidelines or style guides that provide direction on how to use and apply visual elements consistently across various marketing materials and platforms.

- Invest in professional graphic design and visual branding to ensure that your brand assets effectively communicate your brand's identity and differentiate your business in the marketplace.

6. **Build Brand Experience and Engagement:**

- Design and deliver a seamless and memorable brand experience across all customer touchpoints, including your website, social media, packaging, customer service, and physical locations (if applicable).

- Foster meaningful interactions and engagement with your audience through storytelling, content marketing, community-building, and experiential marketing initiatives.

- Encourage brand advocacy and loyalty by delivering exceptional products, services, and experiences that exceed customer expectations and inspire word-of-mouth referrals.

7. **Measure and Iterate:**

- Establish key performance indicators (KPIs) and metrics to track the effectiveness of your brand strategy, such as brand awareness, brand perception, customer engagement, and brand loyalty.

- Use data analytics, surveys, and feedback mechanisms to evaluate the impact of your brand strategy and identify areas for improvement or refinement.

- Continuously iterate and evolve your brand strategy based on market trends, customer insights, and competitive dynamics, ensuring that your brand remains relevant, resonant, and memorable over time.

In conclusion, developing a memorable brand strategy requires a systematic approach that encompasses defining purpose and values, understanding the target audience, establishing brand positioning, crafting compelling messaging, designing visual identity, building brand experience and engagement, and measuring and iterating for continuous improvement. By investing time, effort, and creativity in developing a robust brand strategy, businesses can create a distinct and memorable brand that captivates audiences, fosters loyalty, and drives long-term success.

- Designing Your Visual Identity: Logo, Colors, and Branding Elements

Designing your visual identity, including your logo, colors, and branding elements, is a crucial aspect of creating a memorable and cohesive brand that resonates with your target audience. A well-designed visual identity communicates your brand's personality, values, and unique positioning, helping to establish recognition, trust, and differentiation in the marketplace. Let's comprehensively discuss the process of designing your visual identity:

1. Understand Your Brand:

- Start by gaining a deep understanding of your brand's personality, values, mission, and target audience. Consider how you want your brand to be perceived and the emotions you want it to evoke.

- Conduct market research and competitor analysis to identify trends, preferences, and opportunities in your industry and target market.

- Use insights from your research to inform your visual identity design, ensuring that it aligns with your brand's positioning and resonates with your audience.

2. Define Your Logo:

- Your logo is the cornerstone of your visual identity and serves as the most recognizable symbol of your brand. It should be simple, memorable, versatile, and reflective of your brand's personality.

- Start by brainstorming concepts and ideas for your logo, considering elements such as typography, iconography, symbols, and imagery.

- Sketch out rough drafts and concepts, exploring different design directions and variations. Refine and iterate on your designs until you achieve a cohesive and compelling logo that captures the essence of your brand.

- Consider factors such as scalability, legibility, and adaptability across various platforms and media when finalizing your logo design.

3. **Choose Your Brand Colors:**

- Selecting the right color palette is crucial for establishing brand identity and evoking specific emotions and associations. Choose colors that align with your brand's personality, values, and positioning.

- Consider the psychological effects of different colors and their associations with specific emotions and meanings. Choose colors that resonate with your target audience and convey the desired brand perception.

- Develop a cohesive color palette consisting of primary, secondary, and accent colors that work harmoniously together and reflect your brand's identity.

- Test your color palette across different backgrounds, materials, and media to ensure consistency and visibility in various contexts.

4. **Develop Branding Elements:**

- In addition to your logo and colors, develop additional branding elements that reinforce your brand identity and create a cohesive visual language. These elements may include typography, patterns, icons, illustrations, and imagery.

- Choose typography that complements your logo and reflects your brand's personality and tone of voice. Select fonts that are legible, versatile, and suitable for both digital and print applications.

- Create patterns, textures, or graphic elements that can be used as decorative elements or backgrounds in your marketing materials, website, or packaging.

- Incorporate icons, illustrations, or imagery that align with your brand's aesthetic and messaging, reinforcing key brand attributes and values.

5. Ensure Consistency and Coherence:

- Maintain consistency in the use of your visual identity elements across all touchpoints and communication channels, including your website, social media, marketing materials, packaging, and physical locations (if applicable).

- Develop brand guidelines or style guides that outline rules and specifications for using your visual identity elements, including logo usage, color palettes, typography, spacing, and proportions.

- Educate your team members, partners, and stakeholders on your brand guidelines and ensure that they adhere to them when creating or using brand assets.

- Regularly review and update your visual identity to ensure that it remains relevant, resonant, and aligned with your evolving brand strategy and market trends.

6. **Test and Iterate:**

- Test your visual identity elements with your target audience to gather feedback and insights on their effectiveness and appeal.

- Conduct A/B testing or focus groups to evaluate different logo designs, color combinations, or branding elements and determine which resonates best with your audience.

- Use analytics and performance metrics to track the impact of your visual identity on brand awareness, perception, engagement, and conversion rates.

- Continuously iterate and refine your visual identity based on feedback, data-driven insights, and evolving business goals and priorities.

In conclusion, designing your visual identity is a strategic process that involves understanding your brand, defining your logo and colors, developing branding elements, ensuring consistency and coherence, and testing and iterating for continuous improvement. By investing time, effort, and creativity in crafting a cohesive and memorable visual identity, you can establish a strong brand presence that resonates with your audience and sets you apart from competitors in the marketplace.

- Crafting a Compelling Brand Story

Crafting a compelling brand story is essential for establishing an emotional connection with your audience, communicating your brand's values and mission, and differentiating your business in the marketplace. A well-crafted brand story goes beyond product features and benefits to evoke emotions, resonate with values, and inspire action.

Let's comprehensively discuss the process of crafting a compelling brand story:

1. Understand Your Audience:

- Start by gaining a deep understanding of your target audience, including their demographics, psychographics, motivations, needs, and aspirations.

- Identify the pain points, challenges, and desires of your audience, and consider how your brand can address these needs and add value to their lives.

- Tailor your brand story to resonate with the emotions, values, and interests of your audience, fostering a sense of empathy and connection.

2. Define Your Brand Identity:

- Clarify your brand's purpose, values, personality, and unique selling proposition (USP). Your brand story should authentically reflect these attributes and differentiate your business from competitors.

- Identify the key themes, messages, and narrative elements that define your brand identity and contribute to your brand story.

- Consider how your brand's history, heritage, and founding story can be incorporated into your brand narrative to add depth and authenticity.

3. **Identify the Core Elements of Your Story:**

- Determine the key elements of your brand story, including the protagonist (your brand or your customers), the setting (the context or environment in which your brand operates), the conflict or challenge (the problem your brand solves), and the resolution or transformation (the outcome or solution provided by your brand).

- Use storytelling techniques such as character development, plot structure, and narrative arc to engage your audience and captivate their attention.

- Highlight the emotional journey and transformation experienced by your customers or audience as a result of engaging with your brand, illustrating the positive impact and value created.

4. **Craft Your Narrative:**

- Develop a clear and concise narrative that communicates your brand story compellingly and memorably. Start by outlining the key points and structure of your story, including the beginning, middle, and end.

- Use vivid language, imagery, and sensory details to bring your brand story to life and evoke emotions in your audience. Paint a picture of the world you envision and the role your brand plays within it.

- Incorporate elements of authenticity, vulnerability, and transparency into your brand story, sharing honest insights and experiences that resonate with your audience on a human level.

5. **Communicate Your Brand Story:**

- Choose the most appropriate channels and mediums for sharing your brand story with your audience, including your website, social media, marketing materials, advertising campaigns, and customer interactions.

- Develop a consistent brand voice and tone that reflects the personality and values of your brand, ensuring coherence and alignment across all communication channels.

- Use multimedia formats such as videos, images, infographics, and podcasts to convey your brand story in a visually engaging and interactive way.

- Encourage user-generated content and storytelling by inviting your audience to share their experiences, testimonials, and success stories related to your brand.

6. Iterate and Evolve:

- Continuously monitor and evaluate the impact of your brand story on brand awareness, perception, engagement, and loyalty.

- Solicit feedback from your audience and stakeholders to identify areas for improvement or refinement in your brand narrative.

- Adapt and evolve your brand story over time to reflect changes in your business, market trends, and audience preferences, ensuring that it remains relevant, resonant, and compelling.

In conclusion, crafting a compelling brand story is a strategic process that involves understanding your audience, defining your brand identity, identifying core narrative elements, crafting your narrative, communicating your story effectively, and iterating and evolving. By creating a meaningful and authentic brand story that resonates with your audience's emotions, values, and aspirations, you can build stronger connections, foster brand loyalty, and drive business success in the long term.

CHAPTER 5: SCALING FOR SUCCESS

Scaling a business is a pivotal stage in its journey, representing the transition from a promising startup to a sustainable and successful enterprise. Chapter 5: Scaling for Success delves into the strategies, challenges, and opportunities involved in scaling your business for long-term growth and profitability.

As entrepreneurs embark on the path of scaling, they encounter a myriad of decisions, hurdles, and considerations. From expanding market reach and optimizing operations to scaling team capabilities and managing financial resources, the journey of scaling presents both exhilarating opportunities and daunting challenges.

In this chapter, we explore the key principles and practices that underpin successful scaling initiatives, drawing insights from seasoned entrepreneurs, industry experts, and case studies of successful scaling strategies. Whether you're looking to expand your customer base, enter new markets, diversify product offerings, or streamline operations, this chapter offers practical guidance and actionable strategies to help you navigate the complexities of scaling your business.

Scaling for success requires a holistic approach that encompasses strategic planning, operational excellence, talent development, financial management, and organizational agility. By leveraging the right strategies, tools, and resources, entrepreneurs can overcome the obstacles of scaling and unlock new levels of growth and innovation.

Throughout this chapter, we'll explore the importance of building scalable processes, systems, and infrastructure that can support rapid growth while maintaining quality, efficiency, and customer satisfaction. We'll also discuss the role of leadership, culture, and organizational alignment in fostering a growth mindset and driving sustainable scaling initiatives.

Whether you're a founder leading a high-growth startup or an established business seeking to expand into new markets or verticals, this chapter will provide you with the insights, strategies, and inspiration to scale your business for success in today's dynamic and competitive marketplace.

So, join us as we embark on a journey to explore the strategies, challenges, and opportunities of scaling for success. Whether you're taking your first steps towards scaling or navigating the complexities of growth at scale, this chapter will equip you with the knowledge and tools needed to chart a path to sustainable success and unlock the full potential of your business.

- Mastering the Art of Effective Leadership

Mastering the art of effective leadership is a journey that involves continuous learning, self-awareness, and growth. Effective leadership is not just about managing people or making decisions; it's about inspiring and empowering others to achieve shared goals, fostering a positive work culture, and driving organizational success. Let's comprehensively discuss the process of mastering the art of effective leadership:

1. Develop Self-Awareness:

  - Self-awareness is the foundation of effective leadership. Take time to understand your strengths, weaknesses, values, beliefs, and leadership style.

  - Seek feedback from peers, mentors, and team members to gain insights into how others perceive your leadership approach and areas for improvement.

  - Reflect on past experiences, successes, and failures to identify patterns, learn from mistakes, and refine your leadership skills.

2. Lead by Example:

  - Set high standards for yourself and lead by example in your actions, behaviors, and decisions. Demonstrate integrity, accountability, and professionalism in all aspects of your leadership role.

- Align your actions with your values and communicate transparently with your team, fostering trust, respect, and credibility.

- Show empathy, compassion, and authenticity in your interactions with others, creating a supportive and inclusive work environment.

3. **Communicate Effectively:**

- Effective communication is essential for inspiring and aligning your team towards common goals. Develop strong verbal, nonverbal, and written communication skills.

- Articulate a clear vision, mission, and goals for your team, ensuring that everyone understands their role and responsibilities in achieving them.

- Listen actively to the perspectives, ideas, and concerns of your team members, fostering open dialogue, collaboration, and innovation.

- Provide constructive feedback, recognition, and encouragement to your team, empowering them to grow, learn, and succeed.

4. **Build and Empower Your Team:**

- Invest in building a diverse, talented, and high-performing team that complements your strengths and fills gaps in expertise.

- Delegate authority and responsibility to your team members, trusting them to make decisions and take ownership of their work.

- Provide mentorship, coaching, and development opportunities to help your team members grow professionally and achieve their full potential.

- Create a culture of empowerment, autonomy, and accountability, where team members feel valued, motivated, and empowered to contribute to the organization's success.

5. Foster Collaboration and Teamwork:

- Break down silos and foster collaboration across departments, functions, and levels of the organization.

- Encourage teamwork, knowledge sharing, and cross-functional collaboration to solve problems, drive innovation, and achieve collective goals.

- Promote a culture of openness, respect, and trust, where diverse perspectives are valued, and constructive conflict is encouraged as a means of driving continuous improvement.

6. Adapt and Embrace Change:

- Effective leaders are adaptable and resilient in the face of change and uncertainty. Embrace change as an opportunity for growth, innovation, and learning.

- Anticipate and proactively address challenges, risks, and disruptions, leveraging your leadership skills to guide your team through transitions and transformations.

- Foster a growth mindset and a culture of continuous learning and improvement, encouraging experimentation, agility, and adaptability at all levels of the organization.

7. **Lead with Purpose and Impact:**

- Connect your leadership efforts to a larger purpose and mission that inspires and motivates your team. Communicate the why behind your organization's goals and initiatives.

- Align your leadership actions with the values and priorities of your organization, focusing on creating value for customers, stakeholders, and society.

- Measure and evaluate your leadership impact based on outcomes, results, and the positive difference you make in the lives of your team members and the broader community.

In conclusion, mastering the art of effective leadership is a multi-faceted journey that involves developing self-awareness, leading by example, communicating effectively, building and empowering your team, fostering collaboration and teamwork, adapting to change, and leading with purpose and impact. By investing in your personal and professional development as a leader and cultivating a culture of leadership excellence within your organization, you can inspire, empower, and lead your team to achieve extraordinary results and drive sustainable success in today's dynamic and ever-changing business environment.

- Building High-Performing Teams

Building high-performing teams is essential for achieving organizational goals, fostering innovation, and driving business success. A high-performing team is characterized by strong collaboration, effective communication, shared goals, and a collective commitment to excellence. Let's comprehensively discuss the process of building high-performing teams:

1. Define Clear Goals and Expectations:

   - Start by defining clear, measurable, and achievable goals for your team that align with the organization's objectives and priorities.

   - Communicate these goals and expectations to your team members, ensuring that everyone understands their role and responsibilities in contributing to the team's success.

   - Set performance expectations, standards, and metrics to track progress and evaluate success, providing clarity and accountability for team members.

2. Recruit and Develop Talent:

   - Build a diverse and talented team with a range of skills, experiences, and perspectives that complement each other and contribute to the team's collective capabilities.

   - Recruit team members who demonstrate not only technical expertise but also soft skills such as communication, collaboration, problem-solving, and adaptability.

- Invest in ongoing training, development, and mentorship programs to help team members enhance their skills, knowledge, and capabilities over time.

3. Foster a Positive Team Culture:

- Create a supportive and inclusive team culture that values diversity, respect, trust, and psychological safety.

- Encourage open communication, constructive feedback, and collaboration among team members, fostering a sense of belonging and mutual respect.

- Celebrate successes, recognize achievements, and promote a culture of appreciation and recognition for individual and team contributions.

4. Establish Clear Roles and Responsibilities:

- Define clear roles, responsibilities, and accountabilities for each team member, ensuring that everyone understands their specific role within the team and how it contributes to the overall goals.

- Clarify expectations around decision-making authority, communication channels, and escalation processes to avoid ambiguity and confusion.

- Foster a sense of ownership and empowerment among team members, encouraging them to take initiative, make decisions, and drive results within their areas of responsibility.

5. Encourage Collaboration and Teamwork:

- Foster a collaborative and team-oriented work environment where team members feel comfortable sharing ideas, knowledge, and resources.

- Create opportunities for cross-functional collaboration, knowledge sharing, and brainstorming sessions to generate innovative solutions and drive continuous improvement.

- Facilitate team-building activities, workshops, and offsite events to strengthen relationships, build trust, and enhance teamwork among team members.

6. Provide Resources and Support:

- Ensure that your team has access to the resources, tools, and support they need to perform their jobs effectively and achieve their goals.

- Remove barriers and obstacles that may hinder productivity or collaboration, advocating for additional resources or support as needed.

- Provide coaching, guidance, and mentorship to help team members overcome challenges, develop new skills, and grow professionally.

7. Foster Accountability and Performance:

- Establish a culture of accountability where team members take ownership of their work, deliver results, and hold themselves and others accountable for meeting commitments.

- Conduct regular performance reviews and feedback sessions to assess progress, provide constructive feedback, and identify opportunities for improvement.

- Recognize and reward high performance, achievement of goals, and contributions to the team's success, reinforcing a culture of excellence and continuous improvement.

8. **Lead by Example:**

- As a leader, set the tone for high performance by demonstrating commitment, integrity, and professionalism in your actions and behaviors.

- Lead by example in terms of collaboration, communication, accountability, and work ethic, serving as a role model for your team members to emulate.

- Inspire and motivate your team through your vision, passion, and enthusiasm for the work, fostering a sense of purpose and shared commitment to achieving common goals.

In conclusion, building high-performing teams is a strategic process that involves defining clear goals and expectations, recruiting and developing talent, fostering a positive team culture, establishing clear roles and responsibilities, encouraging collaboration and teamwork, providing resources and support, fostering accountability and performance, and leading by example. By investing in the development and empowerment of your team members and creating a supportive and inclusive team environment, you can build high-performing teams that drive innovation, achieve excellence, and deliver exceptional results for your organization.

CONCLUSION

"The Startup Savant: Insider Tips for Launching and Scaling Your Business" serves as a comprehensive guide for entrepreneurs embarking on the exhilarating journey of building and growing their ventures. Throughout this book, we have explored a wealth of insights, strategies, and practical advice gleaned from experienced entrepreneurs, industry experts, and successful startups.

From the initial stages of ideation and market research to the challenges and opportunities of scaling for success, each chapter has provided valuable insights and actionable tips to help entrepreneurs navigate the complexities of entrepreneurship and achieve their business goals. Whether you're a first-time founder launching a new venture or an established business seeking to expand and grow, the insights shared in this book can serve as a roadmap to success.

We have explored the importance of understanding market opportunities, assessing readiness for entrepreneurship, crafting compelling business plans, defining unique value propositions, conducting market research, securing resources, and navigating funding options. Additionally, we have delved into the intricacies of establishing brand identity, mastering effective leadership, building high-performing teams, and scaling for long-term success.

As you embark on your entrepreneurial journey, remember that success is not defined solely by financial metrics or market dominance but also by the impact you create, the relationships you nurture, and the values you uphold. Embrace the challenges, learn from failures, celebrate successes, and continue to innovate and adapt in response to changing market dynamics.

Ultimately, the true measure of success lies in the journey itself—the lessons learned, the relationships forged, and the growth achieved along the way. As you navigate the ever-evolving landscape of entrepreneurship, may "The Startup Savant" serve as a trusted companion, providing guidance, inspiration, and encouragement to help you realize your vision and build a business that leaves a lasting legacy in the world.

Here's to the bold visionaries, the tireless innovators, and the relentless dreamers who dare to defy the odds and pursue their passions with unwavering determination. May your journey be filled with courage, resilience, and boundless creativity as you carve your path to entrepreneurial success. Thank you for allowing "The Startup Savant" to be a part of your entrepreneurial journey. Wishing you all the success and fulfillment in the world.

9 7 9 8 8 8 3 8 6 5 8 1 6